Sun Tzu and the
Art of Fireground
Leadership

B. Aaron Johnson

Table of Contents

Introduction 5

The Art Of War 7

Laying Plans 9

Waging War 13

Attack By Stratagem................................... 17

Tactical Dispositions 21

Energy 24

Weak Points And Strong 28

Maneuvering.. 34

Variation In Tactics 40

The Army On The March 43

Terrain 50

The Nine Situations 56

Attack By Fire 67

The Use Of Spies.. 71

The 4 Principles 77

Preparation... 79

Responsibility 87

Tactics 94

Leadership 109

About The Author 129

INTRODUCTION

The Art of War is the oldest military work in existence. Written in 500 BC, by Sun Tzu, this philosophy on winning wars has become the most read book on military strategy, tactics, and leadership. The ageless principles and fundamentals contained in Sun Tzu's work, though written for war, can be applied to any conflict and can lead to victory in business, politics, leadership, sports, and on the fireground.

I have made reading *The Art of War,* an annual discipline. With each read I gain new insights, clarity, and actionable advice for a given situation. This book has the same effect on all who have read its pages. As I read, this book's application to the fire service and fireground leadership becomes undeniably transparent. *The Art of War* brings out four principles that will lead to success on the battlefield and the fireground. These four principles are:

1. Preparation

2. Responsibility
3. Tactics
4. Leadership

The first part of *Fireground Leadership* contains the full, original text of *Sun Tzu on The Art of War.* The second part of *Fireground Leadership* outlines the four principles and their application to the fire service.

The Art of War

Sun Tzu

LAYING PLANS

1. Sun Tzu said: The art of war is of vital importance to the State.

2. It is a matter of life and death, a road either to safety or to ruin. Hence it is a subject of inquiry which can on no account be neglected.

3. The art of war, then, is governed by five constant factors, to be taken into account in one's deliberations, when seeking to determine the conditions obtaining in the field.

4. These are: (1) The Moral Law; (2) Heaven; (3) Earth; (4) The Commander; (5) Method and discipline.

5, 6. The MORAL LAW causes the people to be in complete accord with their ruler, so that they will follow him regardless of their lives, undismayed by any danger.

7. HEAVEN signifies night and day, cold and heat, times and seasons.

8. EARTH comprises distances, great and small; danger and security; open ground and narrow passes; the

chances of life and death.

9. The COMMANDER stands for the virtues of wisdom, sincerity, benevolence, courage and strictness.

10. By METHOD AND DISCIPLINE are to be understood the marshaling   of the army in its proper subdivisions, the graduations of rank among the officers, the maintenance of roads by which supplies may reach the army, and the control of military expenditure.

11. These five heads should be familiar to every general: he who knows them will be victorious; he who knows them not will fail.

12. Therefore, in your deliberations, when seeking to determine the military conditions, let them be made the basis of a comparison, in this wise: --

13. (1)   Which of the two sovereigns is imbued with the Moral law?

(2) Which of the two generals has most ability?

(3) With whom lie the advantages derived from Heaven and Earth?

(4) On which side is discipline most rigorously enforced?

(5) Which army is stronger

(6) On which side are officers and men more highly

trained?

(7)   In which army is there the greater constancy both in reward and punishment?

14. By means of these seven considerations I can forecast victory or defeat.

15. The general that hearkens to my counsel and acts upon it, will conquer: --let such a one be retained in command! The general that hearkens not to my counsel nor acts upon it, will suffer defeat: --let such a one be dismissed!

16. While heading the profit of my counsel, avail yourself also of any helpful circumstances over and beyond the ordinary rules.

17. According as circumstances are favorable, one should modify one's plans.

18. All warfare is based on deception.

19. Hence, when able to attack, we must seem unable; when using our forces, we must seem inactive; when we are near, we must make the enemy believe we are far away; when far away, we must make him believe we are near.

20. Hold out baits to entice the enemy. Feign disorder, and crush him.

21. If he is secure at all points, be prepared for him. If he is in superior strength, evade him.

22. If your opponent is of choleric temper, seek to irritate him. Pretend to be weak, that he may grow arrogant.

23. If he is taking his ease, give him no rest. If his forces are united, separate them.

24. Attack him where he is unprepared, appear where you are not expected.

25. These military devices, leading to victory, must not be divulged beforehand.

26.   Now the general who wins a battle makes many calculations in his temple ere the battle is fought. The general who loses a battle makes but few calculations beforehand. Thus do many calculations lead to victory, and few calculations to defeat: how much more no calculation at all! It is by attention to this point that I can foresee who is likely to win or lose.

WAGING WAR

1. Sun Tzu said: In the operations of war, where there are in the field a thousand swift chariots, as many heavy chariots, and a hundred thousand mail-clad soldiers, with provisions enough to carry them a thousand LI, the expenditure at home and at the front, including entertainment of guests, small items such as glue and paint, and sums spent on chariots and armor, will reach the total of a thousand ounces of silver per day. Such is the cost of raising an army of 100,000 men.

2. When you engage in actual fighting, if victory is long in coming, then men's weapons will grow dull and their ardor will be damped. If you lay siege to a town, you will exhaust your strength.

3. Again, if the campaign is protracted, the resources of the State will not be equal to the strain.

4. Now, when your weapons are dulled, your ardor damped, your strength exhausted and your treasure spent, other chieftains will spring up to take advantage of your extremity. Then no man, however wise, will be able to avert the consequences that must ensue.

5. Thus, though we have heard of stupid haste in war, cleverness has never been seen associated with long delays.

6. There is no instance of a country having benefited from prolonged warfare.

7. It is only one who is thoroughly acquainted with the evils of war that can thoroughly understand the profitable way of carrying it on.

8. The skillful soldier does not raise a second levy, neither are his supply-wagons loaded more than twice.

9. Bring war material with you from home, but forage on the enemy. Thus the army will have food enough for its needs.

10. Poverty of the State exchequer causes an army to be maintained by contributions from a distance. Contributing to maintain an army at a distance causes the people to be impoverished.

11. On the other hand, the proximity of an army causes prices to go up; and high prices cause the people's substance to be drained away.

12. When their substance is drained away, the peasantry will be afflicted by heavy exactions.

13, 14. With this loss of substance and exhaustion of strength, the homes of the people will be stripped bare, and three-tenths of their income will be dissipated; while government expenses for broken chariots, worn-out horses, breast-plates and helmets, bows and arrows, spears and shields, protective mantles, draught-oxen and heavy wagons, will amount to four-tenths of its total revenue.

15. Hence a wise general makes a point of foraging on the enemy. One cartload of the enemy's provisions is equivalent to twenty of one's own, and likewise a single PICUL of his provender is equivalent to twenty from one's own store.

16. Now in order to kill the enemy, our men must be roused to anger; that there may be advantage from defeating the enemy, they must have their rewards.

17. Therefore in chariot fighting, when ten or more chariots have been taken, those should be rewarded who took the first. Our own flags should be substituted for those of the enemy, and the chariots mingled and used in conjunction with ours. The captured soldiers should

be kindly treated and kept.

18. This is called, using the conquered foe to augment one's own strength.

19. In war, then, let your great object be victory, not lengthy campaigns.

20. Thus it may be known that the leader of armies is the arbiter of the people's fate, the man on whom it depends whether the nation shall be in peace or in peril.

ATTACK BY STRATAGEM

1. Sun Tzu said: In the practical art of war, the best thing of all is to take the enemy's country whole and intact; to shatter and destroy it is not so good. So, too, it is better to recapture an army entire than to destroy it, to capture a regiment, a detachment or a company entire than to destroy them.

2. Hence to fight and conquer in all your battles is not supreme excellence; supreme excellence consists in breaking the enemy's resistance without fighting.

3. Thus the highest form of generalship is to balk the enemy's plans; the next best is to prevent the junction of the enemy's forces; the next in order is to attack the enemy's army in the field; and the worst policy of all is to besiege walled cities.

4. The rule is, not to besiege walled cities if it can possibly be avoided. The preparation of mantlets, movable shelters, and various implements of war, will take up three whole months; and the piling up of mounds over against the walls will take three months more.

5. The general, unable to control his irritation, will launch his men to the assault like swarming ants, with the result that one-third of his men are slain, while the town still remains untaken. Such are the disastrous effects of a siege.

6. Therefore the skillful leader subdues the enemy's troops without any fighting; he captures their cities without laying siege to them; he overthrows their kingdom without lengthy operations in the field.

7. With his forces intact he will dispute the mastery of the Empire, and thus, without losing a man, his triumph will be complete.This is the method of attacking by stratagem.

8. It is the rule in war, if our forces are ten to the enemy's one, to surround him; if five to one, to attack him; if twice as numerous, to divide our army into two.

9. If equally matched, we can offer battle; if slightly inferior in numbers, we can avoid the enemy; if quite unequal in every way, we can flee from him.

10. Hence, though an obstinate fight may be made by a small force, in the end it must be captured by the larger force.

11. Now the general is the bulwark of the State; if the bulwark is complete at all points; the State will be strong; if the bulwark is defective, the State will be weak.

12. There are three ways in which a ruler can bring misfortune upon his army:--

13. (1) By commanding the army to advance or to retreat, being ignorant of the fact that it cannot obey. This is called hobbling the army.

14. (2) By attempting to govern an army in the same way as he administers a kingdom, being ignorant of the conditions which obtain in an army. This causes restlessness in the soldier's minds.

15. (3) By employing the officers of his army without Discrimination through ignorance of the military principle of adaptation to circumstances. This shakes the confidence of the soldiers.

16. But when the army is restless and distrustful, trouble is sure to come from the other feudal princes. This is simply bringing anarchy into the army, and flinging victory away.

17. Thus we may know that there are five essentials for victory: (1)He will win who knows when to fight and when not to fight. (2)He will win who knows how to handle both superior and inferior forces. (3)He will win whose army is animated by the same spirit throughout all its ranks. (4)He will win who, prepared himself, waits to take the enemy unprepared. (5)He will win who has military capacity and is not interfered with by the sovereign.

18. Hence the saying: If you know the enemy and know yourself, you need not fear the result of a hundred battles. If you know yourself but not the enemy, for every victory gained you will also suffer a defeat. If you know neither the enemy nor yourself, you will succumb in every battle.

TACTICAL DISPOSITIONS

1. Sun Tzu said: The good fighters of old first put themselves beyond the possibility of defeat, and then waited for an opportunity of defeating the enemy.

2. To secure ourselves against defeat lies in our own hands, but the opportunity of defeating the enemy is provided by the enemy himself.

3. Thus the good fighter is able to secure himself against Defeat, but cannot make certain of defeating the enemy.

4. Hence the saying: One may KNOW how to conquer without being able to DO it.

5. Security against defeat implies defensive tactics; ability to defeat the enemy means taking the offensive.

6. Standing on the defensive indicates insufficient strength; attacking, a superabundance of strength.

7. The general who is skilled in defense hides in the most secret recesses of the earth; he who is skilled in attack flashes forth from the topmost heights of heaven.

Thus on the one hand we have ability to protect ourselves; on the other, a victory that is complete.

8. To see victory only when it is within the ken of the common herd is not the acme of excellence.

9. Neither is it the acme of excellence if you fight and conquer and the whole Empire says, "Well done!"

10. To lift an autumn hair is no sign of great strength; to see the sun and moon is no sign of sharp sight; to hear the noise of thunder is no sign of a quick ear.

11. What the ancients called a clever fighter is one who not only wins, but excels in winning with ease.

12. Hence his victories bring him neither reputation for wisdom nor credit for courage.

13. He wins his battles by making no mistakes. Making no mistakes is what establishes the certainty of victory, for it means conquering an enemy that is already defeated.

14. Hence the skillful fighter puts himself into a position which makes defeat impossible, and does not miss the moment for defeating the enemy.

15. Thus it is that in war the victorious strategist only seeks battle after the victory has been won, whereas he who is destined to defeat first fights and afterwards looks for victory.

16. The consummate leader cultivates the moral law, and strictly adheres to method and discipline; thus it is in his power to control success.

17. In respect of military method, we have, firstly, Measurement;   secondly, Estimation   of   quantity; thirdly, Calculation; fourthly, Balancing of chances; fifthly, Victory.

18. Measurement owes its existence to Earth; Estimation of quantity to Measurement; calculation to Estimation of quantity; Balancing of chances to Calculation; and Victory to Balancing of chances.

19. A victorious army opposed to a routed one, is as a pound's weight placed in the scale against a single grain.

20. The onrush of a conquering force is like the bursting of pent-up waters into a chasm a thousand fathoms deep.

E N E R G Y

1. Sun Tzu said: The control of a large force is the same principle as the control of a few men: it is merely a question of dividing up their numbers.

2. Fighting with a large army under your command is nowise different from fighting with a small one: it is merely a question of instituting signs and signals.

3. To ensure that your whole host may withstand the brunt of the enemy's attack and remain unshaken - this is effected by maneuvers direct and indirect.

4. That the impact of your army may be like a grindstone dashed against an egg - this is effected by the science of weak points and strong.

5. In all fighting, the direct method may be used for joining battle, but indirect methods will be needed in order to secure victory.

6. Indirect tactics, efficiently applied, are inexhaustible as Heaven and Earth, unending as the flow of rivers and streams; like the sun and moon, they end but to begin

anew; like the four seasons, they pass away to return once more.

7. There are not more than five musical notes, yet the combinations of these five give rise to more melodies than can ever be heard.

8. There are not more than five primary colors (blue, yellow, red, white, and black), yet in combination they produce more hues than can ever been seen.

9. There are not more than five cardinal tastes (sour, acrid, salt, sweet, bitter), yet combinations of them yield more flavors than can ever be tasted.

10. In battle, there are not more than two methods of attack - the direct and the indirect; yet these two   in combination give rise to an endless series of maneuvers.

11. The direct and the indirect lead on to each other in turn. It is like moving in a circle - you never come to an end. Who can exhaust the possibilities of their combination?

12. The onset of troops is like the rush of a torrent which will even roll stones along in its course.

13. The quality of decision is like the well-timed swoop of a falcon which enables it to strike and destroy its victim.

14. Therefore the good fighter will be terrible in his onset, and prompt in his decision.

15. Energy may be likened to the bending of a crossbow; decision, to the releasing of a trigger.

16. Amid the turmoil and tumult of battle, there may be seeming disorder and yet no real disorder at all; amid confusion and chaos, your array may be without head or tail, yet it will be proof against defeat.

17. Simulated disorder postulates perfect   discipline, simulated fear postulates courage; simulated weakness postulates strength.

18. Hiding order beneath the cloak of disorder is simply a question of subdivision; concealing courage under a show of timidity presupposes a fund of latent energy; masking strength with weakness is to be effected by tactical dispositions.

19. Thus one who is skillful at keeping the enemy on the move maintains deceitful appearances, according to

which the enemy will act. He sacrifices something, that the enemy may snatch at it.

20. By holding out baits, he keeps him on the march; then with a body of picked men he lies in wait for him.

21. The clever combatant looks to the effect of combined energy, and does not require too much from individuals. Hence his ability to pick out the right men and utilize combined Energy.

22. When he utilizes combined energy, his fighting men become as it were like unto rolling logs or stones. For it is the nature of a log or stone to remain motionless on level ground, and to move when on a slope; if four-cornered, to come to a standstill, but if round-shaped, to go rolling down.

23. Thus the energy developed by good fighting men is as the momentum of a round stone rolled down a mountain thousands of feet in height. So much on the subject of energy.

WEAK POINTS AND STRONG

1. Sun Tzu said: Whoever is first in the field and awaits the coming of the enemy, will be fresh for the fight; whoever is second in the field and has to hasten to battle will arrive exhausted.

2. Therefore the clever combatant imposes his will on the enemy, but does not allow the enemy's will to be imposed on him.

3. By holding out advantages to him, he can cause the enemy to approach of his own accord; or, by inflicting damage, he can make it impossible for the enemy to draw near.

4. If the enemy is taking his ease, he can harass him; if well supplied with food, he can starve him out; if quietly encamped, he can force him to move.

5. Appear at points which the enemy must hasten to defend; march swiftly to places where you are not expected.

6. An army may march great distances without distress, if it marches through country where the enemy is not.

7. You can be sure of succeeding in your attacks if you only attack places which are undefended. You can ensure the safety of your defense if you only hold positions that cannot be attacked.

8. Hence that general is skillful in attack whose opponent does not know what to defend; and he is skillful in defense whose opponent does not know what to attack.

9. O divine art of subtlety and secrecy! Through you we learn to be invisible, through you inaudible; and hence we can hold the enemy's fate in our hands.

10. You may advance and be absolutely irresistible, if you make for the enemy's weak points; you may retire and be safe from pursuit if your movements are more rapid than those of the enemy.

11. If we wish to fight, the enemy can be forced to an engagement even though he be sheltered behind a high rampart and a deep ditch. All we need do is attack some other place that he will be obliged to relieve.

12. If we do not wish to fight, we can prevent the enemy from engaging us even though the lines of our encampment be merely traced out on the ground. All we need do is to throw something odd and unaccountable in his way.

13. By discovering the enemy's dispositions and remaining invisible ourselves, we can keep our forces concentrated, while the enemy's must be divided.

14. We can form a single united body, while the enemy must split up into fractions. Hence there will be a whole pitted against separate parts of a whole, which means that we shall be many to the enemy's few.

15. And if we are able thus to attack an inferior force with a superior one, our opponents will be in dire straits.

16. The spot where we intend to fight must not be made known; for then the enemy will have to prepare against a possible attack at several different points; and his forces being thus distributed in many directions, the numbers we shall have to face at any given point will be proportionately few.

17. For should the enemy strengthen his van, he will weaken his rear; should he strengthen his rear, he will

weaken his van; should he strengthen his left, he will weaken his right; should he strengthen his right, he will weaken his left. If he sends reinforcements everywhere, he will everywhere be weak.

18. Numerical weakness comes from having to prepare against possible attacks; numerical strength, from compelling our adversary to make these preparations against us.

19. Knowing the place and the time of the coming battle, we may concentrate from the greatest distances in order to fight.

20. But if neither time nor place be known, then the left wing will be impotent to succor the right, the right equally impotent to succor the left, the van unable to relieve the rear, or the rear to support the van. How much more so if the furthest portions of the army are anything under a hundred LI apart, and even the nearest are separated by several LI!

21. Though according to my estimate the soldiers of Yueh exceed our own in number, that shall advantage them nothing in the matter of victory. I say then that victory can be achieved.

22. Though the enemy be stronger in numbers, we may prevent him from fighting. Scheme so as to discover his plans and the likelihood of their success.

23. Rouse him, and learn the principle of his activity or inactivity. Force him to reveal himself, so as to find out his vulnerable spots.

24. Carefully compare the opposing army with your own, so that you may know where strength is superabundant and where it is deficient.

25. In making tactical dispositions, the highest pitch you can attain is to conceal them; conceal your dispositions, and you will be safe from the prying of the subtlest spies, from the machinations of the wisest brains.

26. How victory may be produced for them out of the enemy's own tactics--that is what the multitude cannot comprehend.

27. All men can see the tactics whereby I conquer, but what none can see is the strategy out of which victory is evolved.

28. Do not repeat the tactics which have gained you one victory, but let your methods be regulated by the infinite variety of circumstances.

29. Military tactics are like unto water; for water in its natural course runs away from high places and hastens downwards.

30. So in war, the way is to avoid what is strong and to strike at what is weak.

31. Water shapes its course according to the nature of the ground over which it flows; the soldier works out his victory in relation to the foe whom he is facing.

32. Therefore, just as water retains no constant shape, so in warfare there are no constant conditions.

33. He who can modify his tactics in relation to his opponent and thereby succeed in winning, may be called a heaven-born captain.

34. The five elements (water, fire, wood, metal, earth) are not always equally predominant; the four seasons make way for each other in turn. There are short days and long; the moon has its periods of waning and waxing.

MANEUVERING

1. Sun Tzu said: In war, the general receives his commands from the sovereign.

2. Having collected an army and concentrated his forces, he must blend and harmonize the different elements thereof before pitching his camp.

3. After that, comes tactical maneuvering, than which there is nothing more difficult. The difficulty of tactical maneuvering consists in turning the devious into the direct, and misfortune into gain.

4. Thus, to take a long and circuitous route, after enticing the enemy out of the way, and though starting after him, to contrive to reach the goal before him, shows knowledge of the artifice of DEVIATION.

5. Maneuvering with an army is advantageous; with an undisciplined multitude, most dangerous.

6. If you set a fully equipped army in march in order to snatch an advantage, the chances are that you will be too late. On the other hand, to detach a flying column for the purpose involves the sacrifice of its baggage and stores.

7. Thus, if you order your men to roll up their buff-coats, and make forced marches without halting day or night, covering double the usual distance at a stretch, doing a hundred LI in order to wrest an advantage, the leaders of all your three divisions will fall into the hands of the enemy.

8. The stronger men will be in front, the jaded ones will fall behind, and on this plan only one-tenth of your army will reach its destination.

9. If you march fifty LI in order to outmaneuver the enemy, you will lose the leader of your first division, and only half your force will reach the goal.

10. If you march thirty LI with the same object, two-thirds of your army will arrive.

11. We may take it then that an army without its baggage-train is lost; without provisions it is lost; without bases of supply it is lost.

12. We cannot enter into alliances until we are acquainted with the designs of our neighbors.

13. We are not fit to lead an army on the march unless we are familiar with the face of the country--its

mountains and forests, its pitfalls and precipices, its marshes and swamps.

14. We shall be unable to turn natural advantage to account unless we make use of local guides.

15. In war, practice dissimulation, and you will succeed.

16. Whether to concentrate or to divide your troops, must be decided by circumstances.

17. Let your rapidity be that of the wind, your compactness that of the forest.

18. In raiding and plundering be like fire, in immovability like a mountain.

19. Let your plans be dark and impenetrable as night, and when you move, fall like a thunderbolt.

20. When you plunder a countryside, let the spoil be divided amongst your men; when you capture new territory, cut it up into allotments for the benefit of the soldiery.

21. Ponder and deliberate before you make a move.

22. He will conquer who has learnt the artifice of deviation. Such is the art of maneuvering.

23. The Book of Army Management says: On the field of battle, the spoken word does not carry far enough: hence the institution of gongs and drums. Nor can ordinary objects be seen clearly enough: hence the institution of banners and flags.

24. Gongs and drums, banners and flags, are means whereby the ears and eyes of the host may be focused on one particular point.

25. The host thus forming a single united body, is it impossible either for the brave to advance alone, or for the cowardly to retreat alone. This is the art of handling large masses of men.

26. In night-fighting, then, make much use of signal-fires and drums, and in fighting by day, of flags and banners, as a means of influencing the ears and eyes of your army.

27. A whole army may be robbed of its spirit; a commander-in-chief may be robbed of his presence of mind.

28. Now a soldier's spirit is keenest in the morning; by noonday it has begun to flag; and in the evening, his mind is bent only on returning to camp.

29. A clever general, therefore, avoids an army when its spirit is keen, but attacks it when it is sluggish and inclined to return. This is the art of studying moods.

30. Disciplined and calm, to await the appearance of disorder and hubbub amongst the enemy:--this is the art of retaining self-possession.

31. To be near the goal while the enemy is still far from it, to wait at ease while the enemy is toiling and struggling, to be well-fed while the enemy is famished:-- this is the art of husbanding one's strength.

32. To refrain from intercepting an enemy whose banners are in perfect order, to refrain from attacking an army drawn up in calm   and confident array:--this is the art   of   studying circumstances.

33. It is a military axiom not to advance uphill against the enemy, nor to oppose him when he comes downhill.

34. Do not pursue an enemy who simulates flight; do not attack soldiers whose temper is keen.

35. Do not swallow bait offered by the enemy. Do not interfere with an army that is returning home.

36. When you surround an army, leave an outlet free. Do not press a desperate foe too hard.

37. Such is the art of warfare.

VARIATION IN TACTICS

1. Sun Tzu said: In war, the general receives his commands from the sovereign, collects his army and concentrates his forces.

2. When in difficult country, do not encamp. In country where high roads intersect, join hands with your allies. Do not linger in dangerously isolated positions. In hemmed-in situations, you must resort to stratagem. In desperate position, you must fight.

3. There are roads which must not be followed, armies which must be not attacked, towns which must not be besieged, positions which must not be contested, commands of the sovereign which must not be obeyed.

4. The general who thoroughly understands the advantages that accompany variation of tactics knows how to handle his troops.

5. The general who does not understand these, may be well acquainted with the configuration of the country, yet he will not be able to turn his knowledge to practical account.

6. So, the student of war who is unversed in the art of war of varying his plans, even though he be acquainted with the Five Advantages, will fail to make the best use of his men.

7. Hence in the wise leader's plans, considerations of advantage and of disadvantage will be blended together.

8. If our expectation of advantage be tempered in this way, we may succeed in accomplishing the essential part of our schemes.

9. If, on the other hand, in the midst of difficulties we are always ready to seize an advantage, we may extricate ourselves from misfortune.

10. Reduce the hostile chiefs by inflicting damage on them; and make trouble for them, and keep them constantly engaged; hold out specious allurements, and make them rush to any given point.

11. The art of war teaches us to rely not on the likelihood of the enemy's not coming, but on our own readiness to receive him; not on the chance of his not attacking, but rather on the fact that we have made our position unassailable.

12. There are five dangerous faults which may affect a general: (1)recklessness, which leads to destruction; (2)cowardice, which leads to capture; (3)a hasty temper, which can be provoked by insults; (4)a delicacy of honor which is sensitive to shame; (5)over-solicitude for his men, which exposes him to worry and trouble.

13. These are the five besetting sins of a general, ruinous to the conduct of war.

14. When an army is overthrown and its leader slain, the cause will surely be found among these five dangerous faults. Let them be a subject of meditation.

THE ARMY ON THE MARCH

1. Sun Tzu said: We come now to the question of encamping the army, and observing signs of the enemy. Pass quickly over mountains, and keep in the neighborhood of valleys.

2. Camp in high places, facing the sun. Do not climb heights in order to fight. So much for mountain warfare.

3. After crossing a river, you should get far away from it.

4. When an invading force crosses a river in its onward march, do not advance to meet it in mid-stream. It will be best to let half the army get across, and then deliver your attack.

5. If you are anxious to fight, you should not go to meet the invader near a river which he has to cross.

6. Moor your craft higher up than the enemy, and facing the sun. Do not move up-stream to meet the enemy. So much for river warfare.

7. In crossing salt-marshes, your sole concern should be to get over them quickly, without any delay.

8. If forced to fight in a salt-marsh, you should have water and grass near you, and get your back to a clump of trees. So much for operations in salt-marshes.

9. In dry, level country, take up an easily accessible position with rising ground to your right and on your rear, so that the danger may be in front, and safety lie behind. So much for campaigning in flat country.

10. These are the four useful branches of military knowledge which enabled the Yellow Emperor to vanquish four several sovereigns.

11. All armies prefer high ground to low. and sunny places to dark.

12. If you are careful of your men, and camp on hard ground, the army will be free from disease of every kind, and this will spell victory.

13. When you come to a hill or a bank, occupy the sunny side, with the slope on your right rear. Thus you will at once act for the benefit of your soldiers and utilize the natural advantages of the ground.

14. When, in consequence of heavy rains up-country, a river which you wish to ford is swollen and flecked with foam, you must wait until it subsides.

15. Country in which there are precipitous cliffs with torrents running between, deep natural hollows, confined places, tangled thickets, quagmires and crevasses, should be left with all possible speed and not approached.

16. While we keep away from such places, we should get the enemy to approach them; while we face them, we should let the enemy have them on his rear.

17. If in the neighborhood of your camp there should be any hilly country, ponds surrounded by aquatic grass, hollow basins filled with reeds, or woods with thick undergrowth, they must be carefully routed out and searched; for these are places where men in ambush or insidious spies are likely to be lurking.

18. When the enemy is close at hand and remains quiet, he is relying on the natural strength of his position.

19. When he keeps aloof and tries to provoke a battle, he is anxious for the other side to advance.

20. If his place of encampment is easy of access, he is tendering a bait.

21. Movement amongst the trees of a forest shows that the enemy is advancing. The appearance of a number of screens in the midst of thick grass means that the enemy wants to make us suspicious.

22. The rising of birds in their flight is the sign of an ambuscade. Startled beasts indicate that a sudden attack is coming.

23. When there is dust rising in a high column, it is the sign of chariots advancing; when the dust is low, but spread over a wide area, it betokens the approach of infantry. When it branches out in different directions, it shows that parties have been sent to collect firewood. A few clouds of dust moving to and fro signify that the army is encamping.

24. Humble words and increased preparations are signs that the enemy is about to advance. Violent language and driving forward as if to the attack are signs that he will retreat.

25. When the light chariots come out first and take up a position on the wings, it is a sign that the enemy is forming for battle.

26. Peace proposals unaccompanied by a sworn covenant indicate a plot.

27. When there is much running about and the soldiers fall into rank, it means that the critical moment has come.

28. When some are seen advancing and some retreating, it is a lure.

29. When the soldiers stand leaning on their spears, they are faint from want of food.

30. If those who are sent to draw water begin by drinking themselves, the army is suffering from thirst.

31. If the enemy sees an advantage to be gained and makes no effort to secure it, the soldiers are exhausted.

32. If birds gather on any spot, it is unoccupied. Clamor by night betokens nervousness.

33. If there is disturbance in the camp, the general's authority is weak. If the banners and flags are shifted about, sedition is afoot. If the officers are angry, it means that the men are weary.

34. When an army feeds its horses with grain and kills its cattle for food, and when the men do not hang their cooking-pots over the campfires, showing that they will not return to their tents, you may know that they are determined to fight to the death.

35. The sight of men whispering together in small knots or speaking in subdued tones points to disaffection amongst the rank and file.

36. Too frequent rewards signify that the enemy is at the end of his resources; too many punishments betray a condition of dire distress.

37. To begin by bluster, but afterwards to take fright at the enemy's numbers, shows a supreme lack of intelligence.

38. When envoys are sent with compliments in their mouths, it is a sign that the enemy wishes for a truce.

39. If the enemy's troops march up angrily and remain facing ours for a long time without either joining battle or taking themselves off again, the situation is one that demands great vigilance and circumspection.

40. If our troops are no more in number than the enemy, that is amply sufficient; it only means that no direct attack can be made. What we can do is simply to concentrate all our available strength, keep a close watch on the enemy, and obtain reinforcements.

41. He who exercises no forethought but makes light of his opponents is sure to be captured by them.

42. If soldiers are punished before they have grown attached to you, they will not prove submissive; and, unless submissive, then will be practically useless. If, when the soldiers have become attached to you, punishments are not enforced, they will still be useless.

43. Therefore soldiers must be treated in the first instance with humanity, but kept under control by means of iron Discipline. This is a certain road to victory.

44. If in training soldiers commands are habitually enforced, the army will be well-disciplined; if not, its discipline will be bad.

45. If a general shows confidence in his men but always insists on his orders being obeyed, the gain will be mutual.

TERRAIN

1. Sun Tzu said: We may distinguish six kinds of terrain, to wit: (1)accessible ground; (2)entangling ground; (3)temporizing ground; (4)narrow passes; (5)precipitous heights; (6)positions at a great distance from the enemy.

2. Ground which can be freely traversed by both sides is called ACCESSIBLE.

3. With regard to ground of this nature, be before the enemy in occupying the raised and sunny spots, and carefully guard your line of supplies. Then you will be able to fight with advantage.

4. Ground which can be abandoned but is hard to re-occupy is called ENTANGLING.

5. From a position of this sort, if the enemy is unprepared, you may sally forth and defeat him. But if the enemy is prepared for your coming, and you fail to defeat him, then, return being impossible, disaster will ensue.

6. When the position is such that neither side will gain by making the first move, it is called TEMPORIZING ground.

7. In a position of this sort, even though the enemy should offer us an attractive bait, it will be advisable not to stir forth, but rather to retreat, thus enticing the enemy in his turn; then, when part of his army has come out, we may deliver our attack with advantage.

8. With regard to NARROW PASSES, if you can occupy them first, let them be strongly garrisoned and await the advent of the enemy.

9. Should the army forestall you in occupying a pass, do not go after him if the pass is fully garrisoned, but only if it is weakly garrisoned.

10. With regard to PRECIPITOUS HEIGHTS, if you are beforehand with your adversary, you should occupy the raised and sunny spots, and there wait for him to come up.

11. If the enemy has occupied them before you, do not follow him, but retreat and try to entice him away.

12. If you are situated at a great distance from the enemy, and the strength of the two armies is equal, it is not easy to provoke a battle, and fighting will be to your disadvantage.

13. These six are the principles connected with Earth. The general who has attained a responsible post must be careful to study them.

14. Now an army is exposed to six several calamities, not arising from natural causes, but from faults for which the general is responsible. These are: (1)flight; (2)insubordination; (3)collapse; (4)ruin; (5)disorganization; (6)rout.

15. Other conditions being equal, if one force is hurled against another ten times its size, the result will be the FLIGHT of the former.

16. When the common soldiers are too strong and their officers too weak, the result is INSUBORDINATION. When the officers are too strong and the common soldiers too weak, the result is COLLAPSE.

17. When the higher officers are angry and insubordinate, and on meeting the enemy give battle on their own account from a feeling of resentment, before

the commander-in-chief can tell whether or no he is in a position to fight, the result is RUIN.

18. When the general is weak and without authority; when his orders are not clear and distinct; when there are no fixes duties assigned to officers and men, and the ranks are formed in a slovenly haphazard manner, the result is utter DISORGANIZATION.

19. When a general, unable to estimate the   enemy's strength, allows an inferior force to engage a larger one, or hurls a weak detachment against a powerful one, and neglects to place picked soldiers in the front rank, the result must be ROUT.

20. These are six ways of courting defeat, which must be carefully noted by the general who has attained a responsible post.

21. The natural formation of the country is the soldier's best ally; but a power of estimating the adversary, of controlling the forces of victory, and of shrewdly calculating difficulties, dangers and distances, constitutes the test of a great general.

22. He who knows these things, and in fighting puts his knowledge into practice, will win his battles. He who

knows them not, nor practices them, will surely be defeated.

23. If fighting is sure to result in victory, then you must fight, even though the ruler forbid it; if fighting will not result in victory, then you must not fight even at the ruler's bidding.

24. The general who advances without coveting fame and retreats without fearing disgrace, whose only thought is to protect his country and do good service for his sovereign, is the jewel of the kingdom.

25. Regard your soldiers as your children, and they will follow you into the deepest valleys; look upon them as your own beloved sons, and they will stand by you even unto death.

26. If, however, you are indulgent, but unable to make your authority felt; kind-hearted, but unable to enforce your commands; and incapable, moreover, of quelling disorder: then your soldiers must be likened to spoilt children; they are useless for any practical purpose.

27. If we know that our own men are in a condition to attack, but are unaware that the enemy is not open to attack, we have gone only halfway towards victory.

28. If we know that the enemy is open to attack, but are unaware that our own men are not in a condition to attack, we have gone only halfway towards victory.

29. If we know that the enemy is open to attack, and also know that our men are in a condition to attack, but are unaware that the nature of the ground makes fighting impracticable, we have still gone only halfway towards victory.

30. Hence the experienced soldier, once in motion, is never bewildered; once he has broken camp, he is never at a loss.

31. Hence the saying: If you know the enemy and know yourself, your victory will not stand in doubt; if you know Heaven and know Earth, you may make your victory complete.

THE NINE SITUATIONS

1. Sun Tzu said: The art of war recognizes nine varieties of ground: (1)dispersive ground; (2)facile ground; (3)contentious ground; (4)open ground; (5)ground of intersecting highways; (6)serious ground; (7)difficult ground; (8)hemmed-in ground; (9)desperate ground.

2. When a chieftain is fighting in his own territory, it is dispersive ground.

3. When he has penetrated into hostile territory, but to no great distance, it is facile ground.

4. Ground the possession of which imports great advantage to either side, is contentious ground.

5. Ground on which each side has liberty of movement is open ground.

6. Ground which forms the key to three contiguous states, so that he who occupies it first has most of the Empire at his Command, is a ground of intersecting highways.

7. When an army has penetrated into the heart of a hostile country, leaving a number of fortified cities in its rear, it is serious ground.

8. Mountain forests, rugged steeps, marshes and fens-- all country that is hard to traverse: this is difficult ground.

9. Ground which is reached through narrow gorges, and from which we can only retire by tortuous paths, so that a small number of the enemy would suffice to crush a large body of our men: this is hemmed in ground.

10. Ground on which we can only be saved from destruction by fighting without delay, is desperate ground.

11. On dispersive ground, therefore, fight not. On facile ground, halt not. On contentious ground, attack not.

12. On open ground, do not try to block the enemy's way. On the ground of intersecting highways, join hands with your allies.

13. On serious ground, gather in plunder. In difficult ground, keep steadily on the march.

14. On hemmed-in ground, resort to stratagem. On desperate ground, fight.

15. Those who were called skillful leaders of old knew how to drive a wedge between the enemy's front and rear; to prevent co-operation between his large and small divisions; to hinder the good troops from rescuing the bad, the officers from rallying their men.

16. When the enemy's men were united, they managed to keep them in disorder.

17. When it was to their advantage, they made a forward move; when otherwise, they stopped still.

18. If asked how to cope with a great host of the enemy in orderly array and on the point of marching to the attack, I should say: "Begin by seizing something which your opponent holds dear; then he will be amenable to your will."

19. Rapidity is the essence of war: take advantage of the enemy's unreadiness, make your way by unexpected routes, and attack unguarded spots.

20. The following are the principles to be observed by an invading force: The further you penetrate into a

country, the greater will be the solidarity of your troops, and thus the defenders will not prevail against you.

21. Make forays in fertile country in order to supply your army with food.

22. Carefully study the well-being of your men, and do not overtax them. Concentrate your energy and hoard your strength. Keep your army continually on the move, and devise unfathomable plans.

23. Throw your soldiers into positions whence there is no escape, and they will prefer death to flight. If they will face death, there is nothing they may not achieve. Officers and men alike will put forth their uttermost strength.

24. Soldiers when in desperate straits lose the sense of fear. If there is no place of refuge, they will stand firm. If they are in hostile country, they will show a stubborn front. If there is no help for it, they will fight hard.

25. Thus, without waiting to be marshaled, the soldiers will be constantly on the qui vive; without waiting to be asked, they will do your will; without restrictions, they will be faithful; without giving orders, they can be trusted.

26. Prohibit the taking of omens, and do away with superstitious doubts. Then, until death itself comes, no calamity need be feared.

27. If our soldiers are not overburdened with money, it is not because they have a distaste for riches; if their lives are not unduly long, it is not because they are disinclined to longevity.

28. On the day they are ordered out to battle, your soldiers may weep, those sitting up bedewing their garments, and those lying down letting the tears run down their cheeks. But let them once be brought to bay, and they will display the courage of a Chu or a Kuei.

29. The skillful tactician may be likened to the SHUAI-JAN. Now the SHUAI-JAN is a snake that is found in the Ch`ang mountains. Strike at its head, and you will be attacked by its tail; strike at its tail, and you will be attacked by its head; strike at its middle, and you will be attacked by head and tail both.

30. Asked if an army can be made to imitate the SHUAI-JAN, I should answer, Yes. For the men of Wu and the men of Yueh are Enemies; yet if they are crossing a river in the same boat and are caught by a storm, they will come to each other's assistance just as the left hand helps the right.

31. Hence it is not enough to put one's trust in the tethering of horses, and the burying of chariot wheels in the ground.

32. The principle on which to manage an army is to set up one standard of courage which all must reach.

33. How to make the best of both strong and weak--that is a question involving the proper use of ground.

34. Thus the skillful general conducts his army just as though he were leading a single man, willy-nilly, by the hand.

35. It is the business of a general to be quiet and thus ensure secrecy; upright and just, and thus maintain order.

36. He must be able to mystify his officers and men by false reports and appearances, and thus keep them in total ignorance.

37. By altering his arrangements and changing his plans, he keeps the enemy without definite knowledge. By shifting his camp and taking circuitous routes, he prevents the enemy from anticipating his purpose.

38. At the critical moment, the leader of an army acts like one who has climbed up a height and then kicks away the ladder behind him. He carries his men deep into hostile territory before he shows his hand.

39. He burns his boats and breaks his cooking-pots; like a shepherd driving a flock of sheep, he drives his men this way and that, and nothing knows whither he is going.

40. To muster his host and bring it into danger:--this may be termed the business of the general.

41. The different measures suited to the nine varieties of ground; the expediency of aggressive or defensive tactics; and the fundamental laws of human nature: these are things that must most certainly be studied.

42. When invading hostile territory, the general principle is, that penetrating deeply brings cohesion; penetrating but a short way means dispersion.

43. When you leave your own country behind, and take your army across neighborhood territory, you find yourself on critical ground. When there are means of communication on all four sides, the ground is one of intersecting highways.

44. When you penetrate deeply into a country, it is serious ground. When you penetrate but a little way, it is facile ground.

45. When you have the enemy's strongholds on your rear, and narrow passes in front, it is hemmed-in ground. When there is no place of refuge at all, it is desperate ground.

46. Therefore, on dispersive ground, I would inspire my men with unity of purpose. On facile ground, I would see that there is close connection between all parts of my army.

47. On contentious ground, I would hurry up my rear.

48. On open ground, I would keep a vigilant eye on my defenses. On ground of intersecting highways, I would consolidate my alliances.

49. On serious ground, I would try to ensure a continuous stream of supplies. On difficult ground, I would keep pushing on along the road.

50. On hemmed-in ground, I would block any way of retreat. On desperate ground, I would proclaim to my soldiers the hopelessness of saving their lives.

51. For it is the soldier's disposition to offer an obstinate resistance when surrounded, to fight hard when he cannot help himself, and to obey promptly when he has fallen into danger.

52. We cannot enter into alliance with neighboring princes until we are acquainted with their designs. We are not fit to lead an army on the march unless we are familiar with the face of the country--its mountains and forests, its pitfalls and precipices, its marshes and swamps. We shall be unable to turn natural advantages to account unless we make use of local guides.

53. To be ignored of any one of the following four or five principles does not befit a warlike prince.

54. When a warlike prince attacks a powerful state, his generalship shows itself in preventing the concentration of the enemy's forces. He overawes his opponents, and their allies are prevented from joining against him.

55. Hence he does not strive to ally himself with all and sundry, nor does he foster the power of other states. He carries out his own secret designs, keeping his antagonists in awe. Thus he is able to capture their cities and overthrow their kingdoms.

56. Bestow rewards without regard to rule, issue orders without regard to previous arrangements; and you will be able to handle a whole army as though you had to do with but a single man.

57. Confront your soldiers with the deed itself; never let them know your design. When the outlook is bright, bring it before their eyes; but tell them nothing when the situation is gloomy.

58. Place your army in deadly peril, and it will survive; plunge it into desperate straits, and it will come off in safety.

59. For it is precisely when a force has fallen into harm's way that is capable of striking a blow for victory.

60. Success in warfare is gained by carefully accommodating ourselves to the enemy's purpose.

61. By persistently hanging on the enemy's flank, we shall succeed in the long run in killing the commander-in-chief.

62. This is called ability to accomplish a thing by sheer cunning.

63. On the day that you take up your command, block the frontier passes, destroy the official tallies, and stop the passage of all emissaries.

64. Be stern in the council-chamber, so that you may control the situation.

65. If the enemy leaves a door open, you must rush in.

66. Forestall your opponent by seizing what he holds dear, and subtly contrive to time his arrival on the ground.

67. Walk in the path defined by rule, and accommodate yourself to the enemy until you can fight a decisive battle.

68. At first, then, exhibit the coyness of a maiden, until the enemy gives you an opening; afterwards emulate the rapidity of a running hare, and it will be too late for the enemy to oppose you.

ATTACK BY FIRE

1. Sun Tzu said: There are five ways of attacking with fire. The first is to burn soldiers in their camp; the second is to burn stores; the third is to burn baggage trains; the fourth is to burn arsenals and magazines; the fifth is to hurl dropping fire amongst the enemy.

2. In order to carry out an attack, we must have means available. the material for raising fire should always be kept in readiness.

3. There is a proper season for making attacks with fire, and special days for starting a conflagration.

4. The proper season is when the weather is very dry; the special days are those when the moon is in the constellations of the Sieve, the Wall, the Wing or the Cross-bar; for these four are all days of rising wind.

5. In attacking with fire, one should be prepared to meet five possible developments:

6. (1) When fire breaks out inside to enemy's camp, respond at once with an attack from without.

7. (2) If there is an outbreak of fire, but the enemy's soldiers remain quiet, bide your time and do not attack.

8. (3) When the force of the flames has reached its height, follow it up with an attack, if that is practicable; if not, stay where you are.

9. (4) If it is possible to make an assault with fire from without, do not wait for it to break out within, but deliver your attack at a favorable moment.

10. (5) When you start a fire, be to windward of it. Do not attack from the leeward.

11. A wind that rises in the daytime lasts long, but a night breeze soon falls.

12. In every army, the five developments connected with fire must be known, the movements of the stars calculated, and a watch kept for the proper days.

13. Hence those who use fire as an aid to the attack show intelligence; those who use water as an aid to the attack gain an accession of strength.

14. By means of water, an enemy may be intercepted, but not robbed of all his belongings.

15. Unhappy is the fate of one who tries to win his battles and succeed in his attacks without cultivating the spirit of enterprise; for the result is waste of time and general stagnation.

16. Hence the saying: The enlightened ruler lays his plans well ahead; the good general cultivates his resources.

17. Move not unless you see an advantage; use not your troops unless there is something to be gained; fight not unless the position is critical.

18. No ruler should put troops into the field merely to gratify his own spleen; no general should fight a battle simply out of pique.

19. If it is to your advantage, make a forward move; if not, stay where you are.

20. Anger may in time change to gladness; vexation may be succeeded by content.

21. But a kingdom that has once been destroyed can never come again into being; nor can the dead ever be brought back to life.

22. Hence the enlightened ruler is heedful, and the good general full of caution. This is the way to keep a country at peace and an army intact.

THE USE OF SPIES

1. Sun Tzu said: Raising a host of a hundred thousand men and marching them great distances entails heavy loss on the people and a drain on the resources of the State. The daily expenditure will amount to a thousand ounces of silver. There will be commotion at home and abroad, and men will drop down exhausted on the highways. As many as seven hundred thousand families will be impeded in their labor.

2. Hostile armies may face each other for years, striving for the victory which is decided in a single day. This being so, to remain in ignorance of the enemy's condition simply because one grudges the outlay of a hundred ounces of silver in honors and emoluments, is the height of inhumanity.

3. One who acts thus is no leader of men, no present help to his sovereign, no master of victory.

4. Thus, what enables the wise sovereign and the good general to strike and conquer, and achieve things beyond the reach of ordinary men, is FOREKNOWLEDGE.

5. Now this foreknowledge cannot be elicited from spirits; it cannot be obtained inductively from experience, nor by any deductive calculation.

6. Knowledge of the enemy's dispositions can only be obtained from other men.

7. Hence the use of spies, of whom there are five classes: (1)local spies; (2) inward spies; (3)converted spies; (4)doomed spies; (5)surviving spies.

8. When these five kinds of spy are all at work, none can discover the secret system. This is called "divine manipulation of the threads." It is the sovereign's most precious faculty.

9. Having LOCAL SPIES means employing the services of the inhabitants of a district.

10. Having INWARD SPIES, making use of officials of the enemy.

11. Having CONVERTED SPIES, getting hold of the enemy's spies and using them for our own purposes.

12. Having DOOMED SPIES, doing certain things openly for purposes of deception, and allowing our spies to know of them and report them to the enemy.

13. SURVIVING SPIES, finally, are those who bring back news from the enemy's camp.

14. Hence it is that which none in the whole army are more intimate relations to be maintained than with spies. None should be more liberally rewarded. In no other business should greater secrecy be preserved.

15. Spies cannot be usefully employed without a certain intuitive sagacity.

16. They cannot be properly managed without benevolence and straightforwardness.

17. Without subtle ingenuity of mind, one cannot make certain of the truth of their reports.

18. Be subtle! be subtle! and use your spies for every kind of business.

19. If a secret piece of news is divulged by a spy before the time is ripe, he must be put to death together with the man to whom the secret was told.

20. Whether the object be to crush an army, to storm a city, or to assassinate an individual, it is always necessary to begin by finding out the names of the

attendants, the aides-de-camp, and door-keepers and sentries of the general in command. Our spies must be commissioned to ascertain these.

21. The enemy's spies who have come to spy on us must be sought out, tempted with bribes, led away and comfortably housed. Thus they will become converted spies and available for our service.

22. It is through the information brought by the converted spy that we are able to acquire and employ local and inward spies.

23. It is owing to his information, again, that we can cause the doomed spy to carry false tidings to the enemy.

24. Lastly, it is by his information that the surviving spy can be used on appointed occasions.

25. The end and aim of spying in all its five varieties is knowledge of the enemy; and this knowledge can only be derived, in the first instance, from the converted spy. Hence it is essential that the converted spy be treated with the utmost liberality.

26. Of old, the rise of the Yin dynasty was due to I Chih who had served under the Hsia. Likewise, the rise of the Chou dynasty was due to Lu Ya who had served under the Yin.

27. Hence it is only the enlightened ruler and the wise general who will use the highest intelligence of the army for purposes of spying and thereby they achieve great results. Spies are a most important element in war, because on them depends an army's ability to move.

The 4 Principles

_____

Preparation

Responsibility

Tactics

Leadership

PREPARATION

"Now the general who wins a battle makes many calculations in his temple ere the battle is fought. The general who loses a battle makes but few calculations beforehand. Thus do many calculations lead to victory, and few calculations to defeat: how much more no calculation at all! It is by attention to this point that I can foresee who is likely to win or lose." [I, 26]

Sun Tzu begins his tome by stating that the art of war is governed by five constant factors. These five factors are to be taken into consideration when "seeking to determine the conditions obtaining in the field".

1. **The Moral Law**
2. **Heaven**
3. **Earth**
4. **The Commander**
5. **Method and Discipline**

Sun Tzu says, "the **MORAL LAW** causes the people to be in complete accord with their ruler, so that they will follow him regardless of their lives, undismayed by danger".

79

This is the first essential that must be in place to ensure victory. If the firefighter is being led into "battle" by a chief that is not trusted, each man will go his own way and loss and defeat will be experienced. Or, a new leader will rise up, one without the title, but others will follow him. This creates internal division, which ultimately leads to destruction. A firefighter who experiences a chief not acting in the best interest of his people will not be in accord with him.

Likewise, if our communities and the people we protect are not in accord with our department they will not support the work we do. We must get out, leave the stations, and walk among the community of people that we serve. We must constantly be looking for additional opportunities to add value to our constituents. The most powerful way to combat negative perceptions, is to create positive perceptions.

HEAVEN "signifies night and day, cold and heat, times and seasons." When Sun Tzu wrote of the heavens he was considering the five elements (wood, fire, earth, metal, water), the four seasons, the winds, and temperatures. As a firefighter the "heavens" play a large role in containing and extinguishing a fire. Knowing what is burning (wood, metal, plastics, etc.), the wind direction, humidity, temperature, and time of day is essential in forming a plan of attack for fire extinguishment and rescue operations.

The **EARTH** is comprised of distance, danger, security, open ground, and the chances of life and death. These are the things which are palpable. That which is real and solid. This is the firefighters equivalent to risk versus reward. What are the risks involved? Does the potential reward outweigh the risks? Do we ensure that our policies and procedures are properly prioritized - life safety, incident stabilization, property preservation?

Closely related to the moral law is the **COMMANDER**. This has all to do with the character of the leader. The commander stands for the virtues of wisdom, sincerity, benevolence, courage, and self-control. These are characteristics that any fire service leader, should stand for, and strive to instill in his subordinates. Check yourself. Which of these are you weakest in? Which of these are you strongest in? Cultivate these characteristics in order to be the leader of a victorious crew.

The physical logistics of a department are summed up in **METHOD AND DISCIPLINE**. This is understanding the proper rank structure, and chain of command, maintaining supplies and equipment, and controlling finances. Without proper tools (and their maintenance) any army or fire crew will fail in its fight. Without finances equipment falls into disarray, newest technology cannot be purchased, proper training is not affected, and personnel are not appropriately compensated. Beyond simply managing the available finances, a victorious leader must create new, and evolving streams of income. Typically, this can most effectively be accomplished by taking advantage of every opportunity to serve and provide a service.

"These five heads should be familiar to every general: he who knows them will be victorious; he who knows them not will fail." [I,11] - *Sun Tzu*

In the final chapters of *The Art of War*, Sun Tzu discusses the use of fire as a weapon, and the utilization of spies to bring victory. In war, fire was used to burn soldiers in their camp and destroy supplies, fuel, and weaponry. Sun Tzu makes the point that, in order for fire to be a useful tool, the supplies for creating fire must always be kept available.

"In order to carry out an attack, we must have means available. The material for raising fire should always be kept in readiness." [XII, 2] - *Sun Tzu*

In the modern fire service we have many tools available to us. Tools for the suppression of fire, prevention of fire, and the rescue of victims. However, for these tools to be most effective they must be available and ready to use. As firefighters, it is our responsibility to be aware of the most current tools and tactics for the completion of our tasks. We must know what tools are available. Those tools must be kept ready. The knowledge for using the tools must be kept sharp.

Do we know what tools and equipment is available? Do we know what tools and equipment our specific department/unit has available? Are those tools properly maintained and ready to be deployed when needed?

"The enlightened ruler lays his plans well ahead; the good general cultivates his resources." [XII, 16] - *Sun Tzu*

The act of pre-planning and being aware of the needs of your operation and community, will allow the "ruler" to ensure that the proper tools, equipment, and resources will be available. It is the leader's responsibility to plan and prepare, not just for the current needs of the community and department, but also for the future. The leader must take time to examine and reflect and get a sense of where the community is headed and what its needs will be.

To "cultivate" is to prepare and use, and acquire and develop. We must be cultivating tomorrow's resources today. When tomorrow comes, with its emergencies and needs, it will be too late to prepare and plan, obtain equipment, or train personnel. The leader must look forward and prepare for tomorrow's unseen emergency, right now.

> *"Thus, what enables the wise sovereign and the good general to strike and conquer, and achieve things beyond the reach of ordinary men, is foreknowledge."*
> [XIII, 4] - *Sun Tzu*

The more we know about the communities we protect, the better prepared we can be. The time to learn about new technology, new industrial processes, or new structures or building methods, is not when we respond to it for the first time, but well in advance, in the pre-planning stages.

A key to gaining foreknowledge in our communities is in the relationships that we build. Sun Tzu lists 5 kinds of spies that must be utilized if victory is to be obtained. These 5 types of spies can be applied to the types of relationships that we must foster.

Local spies. Foreknowledge of a community and it's coming needs can be found by understanding the communities history. Building relationships with long-term residents and community leaders is essential. By understanding its history and the goals a picture of the future of the community can be formed. From this picture, plans for future department needs can be determined.

Inward spies. When it comes to new technology, processes, or materials, the representatives and users must be consulted. As leaders we must be secure enough to humble ourselves and know that we do not know every detail about everything. We must turn to the experts in the technology, process, or materials. These experts are passionate about their product, and can tell you every nuance about it. It is the firefighter's job to apply the product knowledge to practical application of fire prevention or fire suppression.

Converted spies. The fire service must look outside of itself in order to adequately plan for the future. We must work collaboratively with other organizations (non-profit, law enforcement, engineering, mutual aid departments, etc.). What do these organizations see in the future? How does the fire department fit into their plan? How do they fit into the fire department plan?

Doomed spies. There are those individuals who seem to have given up. These are the ones who have seen the history, seen plans made (or not), and still experienced failure. These may be the disgruntled ones. In talking to these individuals much can be gained by understanding their mindset, and what they have seen. The 'exit interview' is critical component of human resources. Every leader should engage leaving employees in an exit interview. It is in these exit interviews that the employee will potentially be most honest. The feedback received will show current areas of weakness in the department, and allow proper future plans to be put into place.

Surviving spies. In magazines, books, conferences, and classes the fire service has a wealth of knowledge to draw from. By knowing the stories and lessons learned from those who have experienced what we are experiencing or have been where we are planning to go we can establish foreknowledge of what to expect. It is from these "voices from the future" that we can adequately plan, prepare, and cultivate the resources that will be needed.

RESPONSIBILITY

"Thus we may know that there are five essentials for victory: (1) He will win who knows when to fight and when not to fight. (2) He will win who knows how to handle both superior and inferior forces. (3) He will win whose army is animated by the same spirit throughout all its ranks. (4) He will win who, prepared himself, waits to take the enemy unprepared. (5) He will win who has military capacity and is not interfered with by the sovereign." [III, 17]

Sun Tzu says, "If you know the enemy and know yourself, you need not fear the result of a hundred battles."   Section III, of *The Art of War,* is dedicated to learning how to know yourself and how to know the enemy.

(1) "He will win who knows when to fight and when not to fight."

To this point Sun Tzu provides two guiding principles:

"supreme excellence consists in breaking the enemy's resistance without fighting" [III, 2]

"the highest form of generalship is to balk the enemy's plans" [III, 3]

In these statements Sun Tzu is suggesting a strategy of counter-attack and anticipation of the enemies moves. If our enemy is a fire incident, our counter-attack is fire prevention.

All firefighter's get excited about the fire incident and response. Bring up the topic of fire prevention or building inspections and the mood seems to drop. Fire prevention and pre-planning activities are the most important component of a successful incident response and fire extinguishment.

Sun Tzu states that the "next best [strategem] is to prevent the junction of the enemy's forces". The goal of fire prevention is to keep the four components of the fire tetrahedron - fuel, oxygen, heat, chemical reaction - from coming together.   This is accomplished in engineering structures and plans review, fire inspections and code enforcement, and public education and training.

Knowing the facilities and structures within our community should be of primary importance. Conducting regular inspections and thorough pre-plans will help to identify potential areas of weakness, know what areas pose the greatest fire risk, and create plans for potential incident occurrences. It is through fire prevention efforts that we can know and anticipate our "enemies" potential plan of attack.

(2) "He will win who knows how to handle both, superior forces and inferior forces."

At times your force will be greater than the "enemies", but at other times the "enemies" force may seem bigger. We can be victorious in either case by continuous learning of fire tactics and strategies. By understanding and training in tactics and strategies for all different incident types, sizes, and occurrences we can be prepared to defeat whatever may come.

Does your training program consist of different types of training - hands-on, lecture, tabletop, online, drills, exercises? Do you train on various types of incident occurrences, or is it always the same 2 or 3 scenarios? Do you incorporate "unforeseen circumstances" into your training scenarios (i.e., primary apparatus is unable to respond, tools needed are not working properly, man-power is diminished, etc.)?

The Art of War commentator, Chang Yu, explains, "The secret lies in an eye for locality, and in not letting the right moment slip."

(3) "He will win whose army is animated by the same spirit throughout all its ranks."

Is your department and its members all pulling for the same goal? Are you motivated to work together for a common task? Do your people do what is best for the department as a whole, or is it every man for himself? Are the department goals and "same spirit" regularly communicated throughout the organization?

To get to a level where all are "animated by the same spirit throughout" requires intentionality of both, the individual and department leadership.

3 Ways in Which a Ruler Can Bring Misfortune Upon His Army [III,12]

1. By commanding the army to advance or to retreat, being ignorant of the fact that it cannot obey. This is called hobbling the army.
2. By attempting to govern an army in the same way as he administers a kingdom, being ignorant of the conditions which obtain in an army. This causes restlessness in the soldier's minds.
3. By employing the officers of his army without discrimination, through ignorance of the military principle of adaptation to circumstances. This shakes the confidence of the soldiers.

Be fully aware of the "position" of your people, understand where they are and who they are. Take the time to learn each of your people's strengths, weaknesses, fears, ambitions, concerns, and needs.

In a fire scene situation, the Incident Commander (IC) cannot be in the thick of operations and continue to give orders, he has lost perspective. He must remove himself and see the "big picture", so as not to misjudge and give wrong orders. The fire scene is no place for politics, posturing, or hurt feelings. "You can't handle an army in kid gloves."

To be victorious the leader must put the right people in the right positions. One Sun Tzu commentator states, "If a general is ignorant of the principle of adaptability, he must not be entrusted with a position of authority."

<u>4 People Every Crew Needs</u>
1. Wise man - *delights in establishing his merit*
2. Brave man - *likes to show his courage in action*
3. Covetous man - *quick at seizing advantages*
4. Stupid man - *has no fear of death*

(4) "He will win who, prepared himself, waits to take the enemy unprepared."

Certain victory comes to those who are prepared. Preparation comes by training, exercise, drill, and knowledge of facilities, processes, and equipment. An attitude of "lifelong learning" and "continuous education" should be promulgated throughout your department and personnel.

There is a saying that says, "When opportunity comes, it's too late to start preparing." This can apply to the organization as a whole, and the individual. It is only through continual preparation and improvement that we can be ready for what may come - large scale incident, natural disaster, promotions, additional responsibilities.

(5) "He will win who has military capacity and is not interfered with by the sovereign."

Are you operating in your designated role? Victory can be easily lost when people start to get involved in tasks and activities that are not part of their role or responsibilities. We each have a position to function in and a part to play. It is when we are all working our part that the organization is in sync and great success can be achieved.

Each individual must master his assigned role, before taking on other responsibilities. Too often, people want to skip parts in the middle to get the top. These individuals never excel at any part, often fail to get to the top, and can be destructive to morale and the department as a whole.

"It is the sovereign's function to give broad instructions, but to decide on battle it is the function of the general." - Wang Tzu

TACTICS

"In war, then, let your great object be victory, not lengthy campaigns." [II, 19]

Of primary importance to any war that is being waged is that the cost be counted. In,*The Art of War,* Sun Tzu provides guidance as to what costs of war can be expected. In Section II, Waging War, he details how to count, maintain, keep these costs to a minimum.

Have we counted the real cost of a fire, disaster, or incident within our community? How much does it cost to shut down a section of the community for any period of time? How much could any "lost business" cost? What would be the cost and impact of complete loss of a structure, building, or local business? What is the cost of equipment and agent for successful fire extinguishment? What toll may be taken on the personnel? What would be the economic, political, organizational, legal, or psychological impacts of an incident?

Sun Tzu makes the point that, when fighting, if victory is long in coming, the campaign lasts for a protracted amount of time, the "men's weapons will grow dull and their ardor dampened." As fire service leaders how can we mind this principle? There are four areas in which our personnel could have "their ardor dampened" and limit their effectiveness.

Incident response.

A structure fire or major disaster will result in a prolonged response by firefighting personnel. Our training often consists of a couple hours of spraying water, deploying hand lines, conducting simulated rescues. All done in a non-emergent environment. The reality is, when a major incident occurs multiple operations will have to be conducted simultaneously, without rest, and with limited personnel performing multiple tasks:

- exterior firefighting
- interior firefighting
- search and rescue
- medical care, treatment, and triage

Are our personnel aware of this reality? Are they physically prepared for this? Does our training adequately prepare them for this level of activity? Have we incorporated rehab into our emergency response plans?

Daily activities.

Every department has the many required daily activities that must be completed, and 'routine' operations that must be conducted. These activities may include:

- station clean-up
- equipment inspections
- data entry and paperwork
- issuing of permits
- standby activities

We all understand that these are items that have to be done. However, is everybody contributing to the completion of the work? If the same few individuals are issuing all the permits, doing the station duties, cleaning up all the paperwork, shift in and shift out, eventually they will have "their ardor dampened", and the team environment will start to erode. On extended incidents or standby activities we need to be mindful of the time individuals are out. Perhaps it would be most beneficial to rotate personnel and units to ensure that, if needed, personnel are energized and ready to respond.

Work schedules.

We all have those one or two people that will always work when we ask. So, it becomes easy to just ask those one or two first, and get the spot filled. Are we aware of the hours our personnel are working? We need to remember that the employee that is saying 'yes' to picking up extra hours, is also saying 'no' to some other activities that would require their time. As the leaders of these individuals it is our responsibility to sometimes say, "no, you can't work today, go home".

Everyone seems to enjoy the various firefighter work schedules that abound - 24/48, 48/96, 24/72, etc. Do we periodically evaluate these schedules to make sure they best fit our personnel and operations?

Training.
Repetitive and familiar training material and scenarios can quickly cause our personnel to have "their ardor dampened". With the rise of online training, it has become easy to assign our personnel to simply watch a video or read a slide show and mark it off as completed training. Is this training alone adequate (see above under incident response)? Are our personnel truly learning and being stretched in their knowledge? Officers and personnel must be creative in their training. We need to develop probable scenarios and experiment with alternative approaches. It does take more effort to plan and prepare, but the reward and learning experience will be richer.

"He wins battles by making no mistakes. Making no mistakes is what establishes the certainty of victory, for it means conquering an enemy that is already defeated...Thus it is that in war the victorious strategist only seeks battle after the victory has been won." [IV, 13] - *Sun Tzu*

I do not fully subscribe to the age-old idea that "there is always somebody better" out there. Somebody has to be the best. The best talent. The most knowledgeable. The top performer.

To win battles you have to make no mistakes. The way to make no mistakes is to be the best at what you do. There is a plethora of personal development resources that provide guidance on being the best. A synthesis of this information has shown that the top performers in any industry minimally possess four characteristics.

Focus. Top performers are laser focused on their goal of becoming the best. They partake only in the activities that will support and contribute to their goals. This often means having to say, "no", to other opportunities (even seemingly good ones).

Passion. Top performers are passionate about what they are doing. Their passion for the field, craft, or industry is what drives them to be the best. Passion is what makes a vocation and career more than just a job. Passion is what enables top performers to put in the longer hours, and make the bigger investments into their development and the enhancement of their industries.

Work Ethic. Top performers have a strong work ethic. Those with less natural knowledge, skills, or abilities, can quickly become a top performer by simply working harder than everyone else. Top performers are the best in their field because they are willing to do the hard work.

Giving. Top performers are givers. They routinely give to those around them, and to their industries at large. They freely share of their knowledge and resources. They continuously contribute to the betterment of all around them. They know that by helping others achieve, and become their best, they will achieve their goals as well.

No matter what your aspirations in the fire service may be, these four characteristics can be applied to ensure that you are the best in your field, and mistakes are not made when it matters most.

For example, if you are one of those individuals that loves being a driver/operator, then you should focus on being the best at that skill. Take courses and classes, read, be in the company of others who are passionate about apparatus operations. You should drive, operate, study, and know the vehicle more than everyone else. Share your knowledge, experiences, and opportunities with those around you. Teach the next generation driver/operator everything that you know, so they are prepared to take the wheel. Transfer your passion to someone else!

"The clever combatant looks to the effect of combined energy, and does not require too much from individuals. Hence his ability to pick out the right men and utilize combined energy...Thus the energy developed by good fighting men is as the momentum of a round stone rolled down a mountain thousands of feet in height." [V, 21,23]
- Sun Tzu

The wise warrior understands that victory cannot be obtained by only one person or type of personality. Victory can come only through the combined energy and talents of the whole team. If more responsibility is placed on one person more than all the others, that individual will quickly tire and 'burn-out'. His effectiveness will become severely diminished. Likewise, if the wrong responsibility is assigned to an unsuited team member, the same results will occur.

Victory comes when the company officer knows his personnel. He knows their strengths, weaknesses, likes, dislikes, experiences, limits, and personal factors. By intimately knowing all personnel, the proper tasks and work loads can be assigned. This utilization of "combined energy" will lead to victory. There are a variety of tools and resources for discovering personality types and individual strengths and weaknesses.

Tu Mu, a Sun Tzu commentator, says, "He first of all considers the power of his army in the bulk; afterwards he takes individual talent into account, and uses each man according to his capabilities. He does not demand perfection from the untalented." Notice how he states that perfection cannot be demanded from the untalented. The inverse of this would be that perfection is to be expected from the talented, the top performers.

"Carefully compare the opposing army with your own, so that you may know where strength is superabundant and where it is deficient." [VI, 24] - *Sun Tzu*

Special operations forces utilizes a peer review assessment tool. This tool is an evaluation by personnel of their peers. With this tool each individual's contributions and skill level can be seen. Areas for improvement can be customized for each individual as their part pertains to the team.

Evaluate your team on a regular basis. An evaluation can be used to understand the level that your personnel are at, where their strengths lie, and what deficiencies need to be worked on. If you find that certain fire or medical skills are lacking you can train on those. If familiarity with specific processes or buildings is needed, then you can arrange for hands-on or walk-throughs to improve in these areas. Any area of deficiency (knowledge, skills, or abilities) is the area where failure should be expected. Ensuring that there are no deficient areas can make your success sure.

Sun Tzu states that there are three areas that must be studied in order to ensure victory in battle.

1. **The different measures suited to the nine varieties of ground**
2. **The expediency of aggressive or defensive tactics**
3. **The fundamental laws of human nature**

In Section XI, The Nine Situations, Sun Tzu lists nine varieties of ground, or situations, and describes the appropriate tactics and how human nature will want to respond to each. Though Sun Tzu speaks of these in relation to troops in battle, they aptly apply to firefighters emergency response and firefighting tactics.

The nine varieties of ground, or situations that personnel may find themselves in are:

1. **Dispersive ground**
2. **Facile ground**
3. **Contentious ground**
4. **Open ground**
5. **Intersecting highways**
6. **Serious ground**
7. **Difficult ground**
8. **Hemmed in ground**
9. **Desperate ground**

Dispersive ground. *"When a chieftain is fighting in his own territory, it is dispersive ground."* [XI, 2] Sun Tzu refers to this as dispersive ground, because the troops are fighting close to home and human nature wills them to back down from the fight, return to their homes, and take care of their own.

We see this played out in the fact that many fire departments will not assign personnel to stations that live within their first-due response area. In South Florida, we can see this tendency demonstrated during an impending hurricane landfall. We must take care of our own homes and families, however, we may not be with them during the storm. We must report to work to serve our communities, as we have promised we would.

In these situations the tactics should be to "fight not". Avoid battle, and shore up a strong defensive position. The leadership should drive and inspire the personnel with unity of purpose. Remind the 'troops' why they serve, the oath they have taken, and their value to the community as a whole.

Facile ground. *"When he has penetrated into hostile territory, but to no great distance, it is facile ground."* [XI, 3] This is the point where the troops are getting into the "thick" of the battle, but have not made a full commitment. They have a "facility for retreating". The point of no return has not been reached. Perhaps this best applies to the start of a large structure fire. The attack begins, but suddenly seems overwhelming and pointless. The tactics employed in this situation should be aggressive, fire service would refer to this as an offensive attack. Do not stop the operation, continue on. The key for victory in this situation is to maintain close connection between all parts of the troops and command. Maintain open communication. Sun Tzu states that this will "prevent desertion" and guard against "sudden attack". When all personnel are watching each others back and maintaining open communication there is no room for anyone to fall back. Working together the goal can be achieved.

Contentious ground. *"Ground the possession of which imports great advantage to either side, is contentious ground."* [XI, 4] This is ground to be contended for. It is in the contentious ground situation that the few and weak can defeat the many and strong. These situations dictate a more defensive posture, "attack not". The tactic used should be first to occupy an advantageous position, hurry up the rear so no stragglers are left behind, and advance with speed without hesitation. In ARFF, fewer personnel (maybe only 1 man and truck) are expected to extinguish large fires and save lives. This can only be accomplished by viewing these situations as contentious ground and applying the advice given here, by Sun Tzu. Know what positions are the most advantageous (staging areas, approaches, etc.) and get to them before the incident does. Use all your resources and work quickly.

Open ground. *"Ground on which each side has liberty of movement."* [XI, 5] On open ground do not attempt to block the enemy's way. This will expose the troops to risk. Take up a defensive position and monitor the defensive tactics in progress. No fire department tries to stop an advancing fire by standing directly in its path. Think especially of a wildland fire. Instead, they defend and protect surrounding exposures, forecast the fires behavior, and adjust tactics accordingly.

Intersecting highways. *"Ground which forms the key to three contiguous states, so that he who occupies it first has most of the Empire at his command, is a ground of intersecting highways."* [XI, 6] The first force to occupy the ground gains command and control. This refers to the formation of alliances and consolidation of forces. Fire departments practice this with the use of mutual aid agreements, and utilization of the Incident Command System (ICS) on large incidents. It is only through these mutually beneficial partnerships and alliances that we can increase the resources available to defend our communities in a time of crisis.

Serious ground. *"When an army has penetrated into the heart of a hostile country, leaving a number of fortified cities in its rear, it is serious ground."* [XI, 7] The troops are in the heart of enemy territory, surrounded by the enemy. Sun Tzu says the troops should forage and plunder to maintain a continuous stream of supplies. This creates an aggressive/offensive position. Maintaining a steady stream of resources is vital to any emergency operation. When working in a fire, maintaining an adequate water supply is critical. When responding to some natural disaster, maintaining a steady supply of items essential to life (water, food, medical care, etc.) is critical to maintaining order and preventing chaos. If the resources fail to make it to the troops, the enemy gains ground, the troops fall back, and victory is lost.

Difficult ground. *"Mountain forests, rugged steeps, marshes and fens - all country that is hard to traverse: this is difficult ground."* [XI, 8] In these situations keep steadily on the march, do not stop or encamp. Keep pushing along the road. Difficult ground requires an aggressive offensive tactic. It will be nearly impossible to restart, once the forward momentum is stopped. Remember back to the physical agility test (or, CPAT) for entrance into the fire academy. By the end of the physical routine, exhaustion was setting in. However, those who stopped before completion, rarely were able to complete the test. The key was to keep pushing, through the exhaustion, all the way to the end.

Hemmed in ground. *"Ground which is reached through narrow gorges, and from which we can only retire by tortuous paths, so that a small number of the enemy would suffice to crush a large body of our men: this is hemmed in ground."* [XI, 9] These are dire situations that require creative strategies and plans to be devised. Troops must not be permitted to retreat. When the troops start to fall apart the enemy will advance and destroy. Training is critical to the fire service. The way to be ready for hemmed in situations is to train creatively for all types of situations. Firefighters must be aware of the most current firefighting techniques, and self-rescue/survival strategies.

Desperate ground. *"Ground on which we can only be saved from destruction by fighting without delay, is desperate ground."* [XI, 10] Desperate ground differs from hemmed in ground in that escape is not possible. In a military situation, this can occur when troops advance into unfamiliar territory, and become blocked by the surrounding terrain, structures, and advancing enemy forces. All that can be done in this situation is, fight. The use of local guides can prevent troops from getting into these positions. Conducting pre-plans, utilizing experts (such as facility managers or subject matter experts), creating and exercising emergency plans can prevent fire department personnel from encountering desperate situations.

"We cannot enter into alliance with neighboring princes until we are acquainted with their designs. We are not fit to lead an army on the march unless we are familiar with the face of the country - its mountains and forests, its pitfalls and precipices, its marshes and swamps. We shall be unable to turn natural advantages to account unless we make use of local guides." [XI, 52] *- Sun Tzu*

LEADERSHIP

"Now a soldier's spirit is keenest in the morning; by noonday it has begun to flag; and in the evening, his mind is bent only on returning to camp." [VII, 28]

Sun Tzu states that "there is nothing more difficult" than tactical maneuvering. "The difficulty of tactical maneuvering consists in turning the devious into the direct, and misfortune into gain." In Chapter VII, Sun Tzu enters into a broad discourse on how exactly to accomplish this. There are three main points that can be applied to the work we do:

1. **Importance of discipline.**
2. **Use of resources.**
3. **Sharing of victories and rewards.**

"Maneuvering with an army is advantageous; with an undisciplined multitude, most dangerous." [VII, 5] *-Sun Tzu*

In the fire service we are familiar with the term discipline as it refers to organization, structure, and uniform operations. *IFSTA Essentials of Fire Fighting,* describes discipline as "an organization's responsibility to provide the direction needed to satisfy the goals and objectives it has identified."

Discipline is not just the sole responsibility of the organization or the organizational heads. Self-discipline is the responsibility of every individual. In our business where times can sometimes be slow, it becomes easy to slip into complacency, and just complete the minimum tasks and requirements. This is an undisciplined mind. Self-discipline mandates that we constantly work toward improving ourselves, our departments, and our community. Self-discipline is taking it upon ourselves to do the hard work that will make the department better, and push it towards is goals and objectives.

"We may take it then that an army without its baggage-train is lost; without provisions it is lost; without bases of supply it is lost. We cannot enter into alliances until we are acquainted with the designs of our neighbors. We are not fit to lead an army on the march unless we are familiar with the face of the country - its mountains and forests, its pitfalls and precipices, its marshes and swamps. We shall be unable to turn natural advantage to account unless we make use of local guides." [VII, 11-14] *- Sun Tzu*

This speaks to the benefit and necessity of taking full advantage of the resources that are available. It is easy to complain about lack of resources, it is easy to request additional funds for more tools, equipment, or apparatus. It takes a bit of 'sweat equity' and creativity to ensure that we are fully utilizing the resources that we have available. This includes those resources that we utilize for training and teaching classes. It also applies to resources that can be used to further our knowledge of the community, facilities, and operational processes.

Your fire prevention personnel can provide a wealth of knowledge in regards to building fire protection and life safety systems. Are you fully utilizing these individuals and extracting as much information out of them as possible? Do you regularly interface and interact with fire prevention to ensure that all personnel have the most current information regarding the facility?

Building and facility managers are experts on the structures they represent. Are you establishing relationships with these individuals? Are you setting up training and tour opportunities with these people for your personnel?

"When you plunder a countryside, let the spoil be divided amongst your men; when you capture new territory, cut it up into allotments for the benefit of the soldiery." [VII, 20] *- Sun Tzu*

No victories are won by a single individual. No fire incidents are successfully addressed without many functioning team members. It takes many people working together, in their particular area, to accomplish victory. When we are rewarded, or receive special mention, we should always pass these onto our team. It is because of the team that we are able to accomplish our stated goals and objectives. There is no room for individuals to only push their personal agenda or build themselves. When the department is functioning as a "united body it is impossible either for the brave to advance alone, or for the cowardly to retreat alone."

"There are five dangerous faults which may affect a general: (1) Recklessness, which leads to destruction; (2) cowardice, which leads to capture; (3) a hasty temper, which can be provoked by insults; (4) a delicacy of honor which is sensitive to shame; (5) over-solicitude for his men, which exposes him to worry and trouble."
[VIII, 12] *- Sun Tzu*

Sun Tzu states that there are **five faults** that lead to an army being overthrown, its leader slain, and a victory lost.

1. **Recklessness**
2. **Cowardice**
3. **Hasty temper**
4. **Delicacy of honor**
5. **Over-solicitude for his men**

Recklessness.

Recklessness leads to destruction. Recklessness is the result of going to battle being ill-prepared and unaware of the opposition. One commentator states, "...he who fights recklessly, without any perception of what is expedient, must be condemned." To go into battle, to attack a fire or approach an incident scene, without any prior preparation or knowledge will result in loss. The way to prevent recklessness is to be always ready, always prepared. Recklessness can be eliminated by constant and evolving training, by fire prevention and pre-planning efforts, and by networking and learning from those that have gone before.

Cowardice.

Cowardice leads to capture. The translation of the Chinese word for 'cowardice' used here refers to "the man whom timidity prevents from advancing to seize an advantage". With the fire department's emphasis on safety, it seems that the "timid" firefighter is becoming more common. Though we must act safely, we must also remember, that we have not chosen a 'safe' career. People are counting on us to do the hard things, to take the risks, that nobody else will. Timidity leads to hesitation which leads to death.

This idea was best stated by FDNY Lt. Ray McCormack during his keynote speech at the 2009 FDIC. In his address Lt. McCormack stated that the fire service needs a "culture of extinguishment not safety". Due to the "constant barrage" of safety messages, the fire service is at risk of losing its identity and effectiveness. If firefighters stop taking the risks necessary to save lives, who will do it? Who will step in to save these lives?

Hasty temper.
A hasty temper can be provoked by insults. This speaks to the importance of self-control. Destruction and loss will surely come to those who cannot control their emotions. When emotions are allowed free reign all perspective, reasoning, and logic disappears. In anger and selfishness we are prone to poor decision making, speaking things which should not be said, and taking part in inappropriate actions. Many careers have been lost due to letting emotions take-over, and not being kept in check.

Delicacy of honor.

Delicacy of honor is sensitivity to shame. This is not to say that honor is a negative quality in a leader. The meaning of this phrase is the victorious leader must be thick skinned. There is no room for sensitivity to outside judgments, slanderous reports, or opinion. Leaders stand by their decisions, and understand what they are ultimately responsible for, regardless of what others may say. A Sun Tzu contemporary stated this sentiment as, "They who seek after glory should be careless of public opinion".

Over-solicitude for his men.

Over-solicitude for the men, will expose them to worry and trouble. The Marine Corps primary objective is, mission accomplishment. Their secondary objective is, troop welfare. At first glance, this may seem out of order. Since troops are needed to complete the mission, shouldn't their welfare be first? The answer is no, and here's why. If we put troop welfare first, then the mission would fail based on the attitude, feelings, or ideas of each man. However, with mission accomplishment being the primary objective, personal feelings, ideas, and discomfort are not a hindrance to victory.

The good leader, or company officer, does not neglect the care of his personnel. He does, however, understand and emphasizes the primary objective of mission accomplishment.

Sun Tzu introduces these five faults with the idea that he has expressed throughout his writing, prevention and preparedness are key to victory. He states, "The art of war teaches us to rely not on the likelihood of the enemy's not coming, but on our own readiness to receive him; not on the chance of his not attacking, but rather on the fact that we have made our position unassailable."

"If there is disturbance in the camp, the general's authority is weak. If the banners and flags are shifted about, sedition is afoot. If the officers are angry, it means that the men are weary...The sight of men whispering together in small knots or speaking in subdued tones points to disaffection amongst the rank and file." [IX, 33,35] - *Sun Tzu*

A sure path to defeat on the battlefield, and the fireground, is lack of disciplined personnel. Recognizing the signs and symptoms of a discipline deficiency is the first step to ensuring victory with your personnel. Sun Tzu addresses four signs and symptoms of discipline deficiency, and four cures for this deficiency. Upon seeing the first glimpses of these signs and symptoms the department heads should seriously examine the department and personnel and make needed corrections.

4 Signs of a Discipline Deficiency

1. Disturbance in the camp
2. Angry officers
3. Shifting of banners and flags
4. Small huddles and subdued tones

Disturbance in the camp. If it seems that the daily operations of the shift just do not go smoothly, or it seems that there is always an 'issue' or 'problem' being caused this is a sign of weakened leadership. The men feel that they do not have to follow the leaders commands. This is the source of the disturbance. Instead of just doing what is asked, the officers and personnel feel that they have the right to question every decision, and treat every order as 'optional'.

Shifting of banners and flags. In war, banners and flags were used to send signals and messages on the battlefield. Shifting of banners and flags indicates that someone else is sending the signals. The troops are following another's orders. Though, the leader by title (lieutenant, captain, chief, etc.) has given the orders, the troops are carrying out the commands of another. This other individual is the person the troops trust, and believe to have their best interests in mind, regardless of formal title.

Angry officers. If the troops are tired, weary, lack motivation, every task becomes a major undertaking, every command is met with resistance. This will quickly wear on the officer's patience. The officer has a command to fulfill, he needs his men to accomplish the goal, when they are not working cohesively it makes the job doubly hard. The officer just wants his people to do the job they are supposed to do. The troops, however, are not at the peak of their performance. They are tired or weary. Their minds are not clear or focused. This is also tied to the point above, if the officers do not have real authority, the men are following the cues of someone else, the officer will feel defeated.

Small huddles and subdued tones. The disgruntled troops will start to form groups (we might refer to them as 'cliques') with those who share the same complaints. They will start to separate themselves from the larger department body. These groups can be like cancer to a department. They start with a few minor complaints, then spread their negativity and bad ideas to everyone else. Often times the disturbance in the camp, is a result of these small huddles.

These four symptoms work in a type of loop system and each is connected to another. If there is a disturbance, a complaint, an uneasiness, a lack of cohesion, the troops start to look elsewhere for leadership. They are looking to the one that can bring the troops, or shift, back together and establish order. The troops see the disturbance as a failure on the officer's part, and do not follow his commands. They break away and start to form their own groups and spread their discontent.

Troops in this condition, that demonstrate these symptoms will not be successful on the battlefield, or on the fireground. Lack of discipline among the troops, will lead to sure defeat.

Sun Tzu, does not just tell the symptoms, he provides the cure.

"If soldiers are punished before they have grown attached to you, they will not prove submissive; and, unless submissive, then will be practically useless. If, when the soldiers have become attached to you, punishments are not enforced, they will still be useless. Therefore, soldiers must be treated in the first instance

with humanity, but kept under control by means of iron discipline. This is a certain road to victory. If in training soldiers commands are habitually enforced, the army will be well-disciplined; if not, its discipline will be bad. If a general shows confidence in his men but always insists on his orders being obeyed, the gain will be mutual." [IX, 42-44] - *Sun Tzu*

4 Cures for Discipline Deficiency

1. Treat men with humanity; control with discipline
2. Habitually enforce all commands (even in training)
3. Show confidence in the men
4. Insist on orders being obeyed

Treat men with humanity; control with discipline.
Treat your personnel well. Make sure to care for their needs. Earn the trust and respect of your people. However, discipline must still be maintained. Ensure that personnel understand the goals of the department, and expectations of its personnel. When personnel act inappropriately or do not follow orders punishment, and corrective action, must be handed out. Rules, policies, procedures, must be enforced. When they are not, the trust and respect earned, begins to erode.

Habitually enforce all commands. Discipline must be maintained at all times. Consistency is what is needed. Even in training, with limited risk, discipline must still be enforced. When officers let things slide during down times and training, it is believed that the officer will always let things slide. The officers leadership will then be compromised. And as long as, personnel feel that they will not be disciplined for disobeying orders, or freelancing, then the whole company is at risk.

Show confidence in the men. Trust your personnel. Do not micro-manage, let them do their job. Also, do not be quick to discipline, have confidence that your personnel did not deliberately disobey an order, policy, or procedure. Investigate, then discipline.

Insist on orders being obeyed. In today's society people seem to get their feelings hurt easily, they want explanations for everything, and they feel entitled to share their opinion on all matters. As the leader, the commands and orders that you issue must be obeyed. Hurt feelings, explanations, and other's opinions do not change this fact.

Terrain refers to the topographical features of a geographical location. To discuss terrain is to discuss the lay of the land. When we are conducting pre-plans for fire and emergency response, the terrain plays an important role. Terrain elements include the location of roads, vegetation, bodies of water, overhead obstructions (power lines, trees, canopies), and exposures. We want to look at how the terrain and surrounding structures will impact fire behavior to the structure, how a structure fire will impact the surrounding terrain and other structures. When assessing exposure hazards - in the sense of what will expose a structure to fire risk - some factors considered are differing building heights, distance between buildings, wildland/urban interface settings, and the proximity of high-hazard operations or contents. The goal is to create a plan to limit risk from these exposures.

As terrain can refer to the physical land layout, as leaders, we establish leadership and cultural terrain with our personnel. Based on how we lead our people we are either creating a culture that exposes them to risk, failure, and defeat or we are creating a culture that will limit their exposure to risk, ensure their personal success, and professional victory.

"Now an army is exposed to six severe calamities, not arising from natural causes, but from faults for which the general is responsible..." [X, 14] *- Sun Tzu*

Sun Tzu, discusses six "exposures" that our personnel could be subject to. These six exposures are, flight, insubordination, collapse, ruin, disorganization, and rout.

Flight.

"If one force is hurled against another ten times its size, the result will be flight of the former." [X, 14]
When an incident - fire scene or management issue - exceeds the the department's assets the personnel involved will feel overwhelmed and defeat will be imminent. It is the leader's responsibility to know the capabilities of his personnel, assets, and resources. Specifically, the leader must know when these are not adequate for the fight. It is the leader's responsibility to know when to request additional assets, provide additional knowledge or human resources, or seek counsel and advice. As leaders, we must be knowledgeable enough to know that we need assistance, and humble enough to request it.

Insubordination.

"When the common soldiers are too strong and their officers too weak, the result is insubordination." [X, 16]
This statement should not be taken to mean that leaders and officers should suppress the development of their people, but just the opposite. It is critically important that the leader works and trains just as much, or more,

than his personnel so that his knowledge and growth will continue and he can be on par with the knowledge, skills, and abilities of his men. As officers and departmental leaders we are expected to lead. We are the ones that have to make the hard decisions and stand by them. When officers do not do this the men will not follow. They will, instead, follow the man who can do this. They will follow the man who does maintain and continually develop his knowledge, skills, and abilities - both, in the practical functions of the job and in leadership skills.

Collapse.

"When the officers are too strong and the common soldiers too weak, the result is collapse." [X, 16]

An officer is only as strong as his people. The officer can be the strongest, smartest, most knowledgeable, best capable, but if his team cannot keep up then defeat will come. Victory cannot be won on the officer's strength alone. To prevent collapse, it is the officer's responsibility to continually make his personnel better. It is the leader's responsibility to bring the people up to and hold them accountable to highest standards of excellence.

Ruin.

"When the higher officers are angry and insubordinate, and...give battle...from a feeling of resentment...the result is ruin." [X, 17]

Sometimes it is easy for officers to get tunnel vision and only think about what they can see from their perspective. The Chief, however, has a larger view and understands all the connecting parts. The Chief's actions and orders are based on facts and his knowledge of the whole picture. When officers become disgruntled with commands they do not understand, or make decisions based on their limited perspective (commonly referred to as, "freelancing"), ruin will come. Chief's can mitigate this exposure by explaining what can be explained, and officers can mitigate this exposure by submitting to their authority.

Disorganization.

"When the general is weak and without authority; when his orders are not clear and distinct; when there are no fixed duties assigned to officers and men, and the ranks are formed in a slovenly haphazard manner, the result is utter disorganization." [X, 18]

An officer's orders must be given with confidence and decisiveness. If they are not, they will not be followed. Every man must know and understand his role on the team, and within the organization as a whole. He should be given clear guidance as to the functions of his position, and how he can attain to other positions. Serious thought and consideration should be given to the makeup of shifts and personnel. The "ranks" should be formed with the right mixture of experience, skill, and personality.

Rout.

"When a general...neglects to place picked soldiers in the front rank, the result must be rout." [X, 19]

This phrase speaks to the importance of putting the right men on the "front lines", having the right people in leadership roles. Our jobs are not easy, sometimes we are faced with large, extended fire or emergency events, we have to make hard decisions, we have to do the hard work of steering the organization. If the weak or timid are on the front lines, then "disorderly retreat", rout, will ensue. Chan Yu paraphrases, "Whenever there is fighting to be done, the keenest spirits should be appointed to serve in the front ranks, both in order to strengthen the resolution of our own men and to demoralize the enemy."

The principles for creating a victorious leadership and cultural terrain can be summarized in these lines from the Sun Tzu:

"The general who advances without coveting fame and retreats without fearing disgrace, whose only thought is to protect his country and do good service for his sovereign, is the jewel of the kingdom. Regard your soldiers as your children, and they will follow you into the deepest valleys; look upon them as your own beloved sons, and they will stand by you even unto death." [X, 24-25] - *Sun Tzu*

ABOUT THE AUTHOR

Aaron has more than a decade of fire service experience. He began his career as an ARFF firefighter moved to driver/operator, then transitioned into fire prevention. He holds multiple fire service and emergency management certifications and serves on multiple NFPA technical committees. Aaron is the author of more than 400 books, articles, reports, white papers, and blog posts on fire service topics. He regularly speaks at industry conferences, and is a member of the International Code Council (ICC), National Fire Protection Association (NFPA), the ARFF Working Group, and the Florida Fire Chiefs Association.

Aaron currently services as Fire Marshal for Rural/Metro Fire in South Florida, where he resides with his wife, Jacqueline, and sons Aidan and Owen.

Aaron's writing, books, resources, and additional information can be viewed at his website, www.TheCodeCoach.com. He can be contacted at, thecodecoach@gmail.com.

www.ingramcontent.com/pod-product-compliance
Lightning Source LLC
Chambersburg PA
CBHW071447180526
45170CB00001B/492